DATE DUE

STECK-VAUGHN
PORTRAIT OF AMERICA

Kentucky

Steck-Vaughn Company
Executive Editor	Diane Sharpe
Senior Editor	Martin S. Saiewitz
Design Manager	Pamela Heaney
Photo Editor	Margie Foster

Proof Positive/Farrowlyne Associates, Inc.
Program Editorial, Revision Development, Design, and Production

Consultant: Ron D. Bryant, Curator of Rare Books, Kentucky Historical Society

Published by Raintree Steck-Vaughn Publishers, an imprint of Steck-Vaughn Company.

A Turner Educational Services, Inc. book. Based on the Portrait of America television series by R. E. (Ted) Turner.

Cover Photo: Cumberland Gap by © Tom Till/Tony Stone Worldwide.

Library of Congress Cataloging-in-Publication Data

Thompson, Kathleen.
    Kentucky / Kathleen Thompson.
       p.   cm. — (Portrait of America)
    "Based on the Portrait of America television series"—T.p. verso.
    "A Turner book."
    Includes index.
    ISBN 0-8114-7337-6 (library binding).—ISBN 0-8114-7442-9 (softcover)
    1. Kentucky—Juvenile literature. [1. Kentucky] I. Title.
    II. Series: Thompson, Kathleen. Portrait of America.
    F451.3.T48 1996
    976.9—dc20   95-40012
                                           CIP
                                           AC

Acknowledgments
The publishers wish to thank the following for permission to reproduce photographs:
P. 7 © James Archambeault/Lexington Convention & Visitors Bureau; p. 8 Kentucky Department of Parks; pp. 10, 11, 12 (both) Filson Club Historical Society; p. 13 Kentucky Military History Museum Collection, Kentucky Historical Society; pp. 15, 16 Filson Club Historical Society; pp. 18, 19 A. D. Porter and Sons Funeral Home, Inc.; p. 20 © Superstock; p. 22 (top) KFC Corporation, (bottom) GM Corporation, Bowling Green Plant; p. 23 Maker's Mark Distillery; p. 24 (top) Kentucky Department of Travel Development, (bottom) © James Archambeault/Lexington Convention & Visitors Bureau; p. 25 KFC Corporation; p. 27 UPI/Bettmann; pp. 28, 29 (both) Taylor Made Sales Agency; p. 30 © Mark Gibson/Southern Stock; p. 32 (both) Berea College Appalachian Museum; p. 33 Kentucky Department of Parks; p. 34 © Michael Lawrence/John James Audubon Museum; p. 35 Kentucky Horse Park; p. 37 © George Pickow; p. 38 © Jim DeVault/Buddy Lee Attractions Inc.; p. 39 (top) © George Pickow, (bottom) © Russ Harrington; pp. 40, 41 (both) Chip Clark/Mammoth Cave National Park; p. 42 © Superstock; p. 44 Louisville Convention & Visitors Bureau; p. 46 One Mile Up; p. 47 (left) One Mile Up, (center, right) Kentucky Department of Travel.

STECK-VAUGHN
PORTRAIT OF AMERICA

Kentucky

Kathleen Thompson

A Turner Book

RSVP

RAINTREE
STECK-VAUGHN
PUBLISHERS
The Steck-Vaughn Company

Austin, Texas

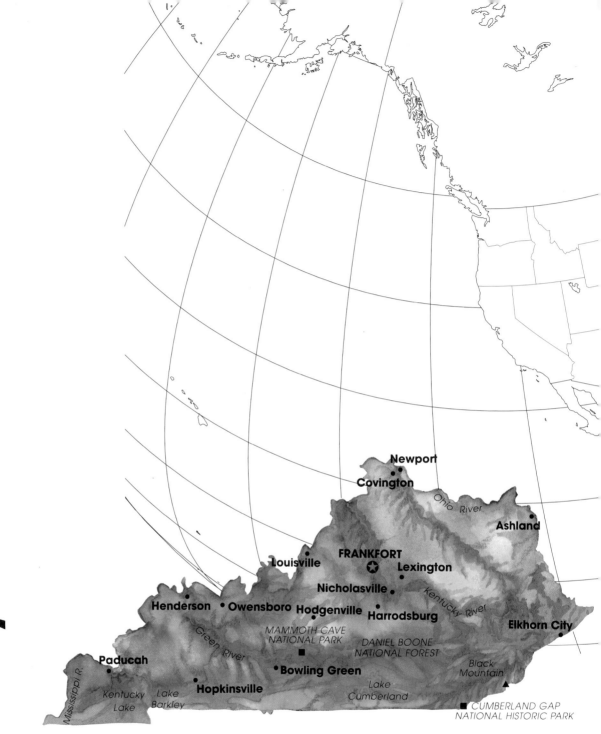

Kentucky

Newport
Covington
Ohio River
Ashland
FRANKFORT
Louisville
Lexington
Nicholasville
Kentucky River
Henderson • Owensboro Hodgenville • Harrodsburg
MAMMOTH CAVE
NATIONAL PARK
DANIEL BOONE
NATIONAL FOREST
Elkhorn City
Green River
Black
Mountain
Paducah
Bowling Green
Lake
Cumberland
Mississippi R.
Hopkinsville
Kentucky
Lake
Lake
Barkley
CUMBERLAND GAP
NATIONAL HISTORIC PARK

Contents

Introduction

Kentucky is the Bluegrass State. Acres of rolling bluegrass pasturelands provide nourishment for the state's champion thoroughbred racehorses. Bluegrass music has the whole state humming with the sounds of fiddles, banjos, and melodic harmonies. Bluegrass has brought fame to Kentucky. But it is the people who have contributed the most to the state. The bold settlers of the frontier land have set an example for the modern pioneers; they are carving their niche in the new century.

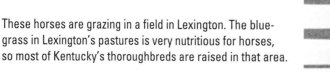

These horses are grazing in a field in Lexington. The bluegrass in Lexington's pastures is very nutritious for horses, so most of Kentucky's thoroughbreds are raised in that area.

Kentucky

Kentucky: Bold and Determined

Once the land we now call Kentucky was part of a great hunting ground. The towering trees, the lush undergrowth, and the crystal streams were home to an abundance of animals, birds, and fish. Surrounding the hunting ground were settlements of five Native American nations: Cherokee, Chickasaw, Wyandot, Delaware, and Shawnee. These groups made an agreement not to live on the land they shared for food. Instead the hunters made trips to bring food and furs back to their people. The Native Americans prospered by this arrangement, even though they sometimes fought over hunting territories.

The first Europeans to come into the area included the English explorers Abram Wood, Gabriel Arthur, and John Peter Salley. French explorers Jacques Marquette, Louis Jolliet, and René-Robert Cavelier, Sieur de La Salle, also passed through. In 1750 Dr. Thomas Walker discovered a route through the Cumberland Mountains. He called it the Cumberland

Daniel Boone founded Boonesborough in 1775 by the Kentucky River.

9

Gap. Dr. Walker traveled as far as the Cumberland River before returning to Virginia.

One of the best-known explorers to arrive through the gap was the legendary Daniel Boone. He made his first trip to Kentucky in 1767. Two years later he came back with a group of hunters.

Daniel Boone and the other explorers saw the Native American hunting ground as unclaimed land. In 1773 Boone brought a group of settlers into Kentucky. But the Native Americans made them turn around and go back.

The Native Americans could not keep the settlers and explorers from intruding on their land, however. In 1774 some Native American groups signed a treaty giving up their rights to all land south of the Ohio River. It was an effort to keep at least part of their hunting ground. The area given up included the hunting ground that now is Kentucky. Also in 1774, James Harrod established the first permanent European settlement in Kentucky. The next year, Daniel Boone founded a fort on the south bank of the Kentucky River. The fort was called Boonesborough.

However, there were still Native Americans who had not given away or sold the rights to their hunting grounds. These groups no longer tried to lead the settlers peacefully out of their land. They began to fight.

Daniel Boone was a courageous leader who helped establish the first permanent settlements in Kentucky.

In 1776 Kentucky became a county of Virginia, and settlers began to move into the area. The settlers had a problem, however. They were separated from the rest of Virginia by high mountains and dense forests. That meant they had to defend themselves against Native American attacks. The settlers received little help from outside. The Native Americans, who were friendly with the British, used British artillery in their repeated attacks. Daniel Boone, Simon Kenton, and George Rogers Clark defended the settlements as best they could.

In 1778 Clark led a force of several hundred men against three British forts northwest of Kentucky. These forts, defended by Native Americans and French and British troops, held British military supplies. Clark and his men captured Vincennes, in what is now Indiana, and Kaskaskia and Cahokia, in present-day Illinois. These victories cut the British supply lines. As a result, Native American attacks on

The State House in Frankfort was built in 1795 and burned in 1813 during the War of 1812 against the British.

Kentucky settlers became much less frequent. After about four years, they stopped almost completely.

Because Kentucky settlers had received so little help during the Revolutionary War, they no longer wanted to be part of the Virginia colony. In 1784 the settlers held a convention at Danville to consider separating from Virginia. Kentucky became the fifteenth state in 1792. Frankfort was selected as the state capital.

In the years that followed, more land was opened to settlement. Kentucky increased its population from about 75,000 to more than 1 million. Kentucky's rich grasslands provided perfect grazing conditions for raising horses. Horse breeding soon became popular in central Kentucky. Kentucky farmers grew mainly hemp, tobacco, and cotton. As in many other southern

Workers on a Kentucky farm spread hemp to dry. Before the Civil War, hemp was the state's most valuable crop.

states, plantation owners brought in African slaves to work in the fields.

In 1803 the United States bought all of the land known as the Louisiana Territory from France. This land ranged from the Mississippi River to the Rocky Mountains and from the Gulf of Mexico to the Canadian border. For Kentuckians the purchase opened up a market for its farm products downstream along the Mississippi River.

Confederate forces were defeated at the Battle of Mill Springs in southern Kentucky on January 19, 1862.

Two main issues led up to the Civil War. One of the issues was slavery. The other was states' rights, or the amount of control the federal government had over the states. The people of Kentucky were divided over these issues. The powerful plantation owners sided with the Confederacy, which was proslavery and pro-states' rights. The plantation owners were angry because the Kentucky legislature passed a law in 1833 forbidding the importation of any more slaves. Other Kentuckians sided with the Union. Kentucky, which bordered the South, tried without success to remain neutral. More than seventy thousand men from Kentucky fought for the Union. More than thirty thousand fought for the Confederacy.

Only after the war did Kentucky become strongly sympathetic to the South. The period 1865 to 1877, following the Civil War, was called Reconstruction. During this time the United States set about a process by which the states of the Confederacy were readmitted to full membership in the Union. Some of the laws passed by the federal government during Reconstruction imposed harsh penalties on the South. Kentucky suffered from these laws and developed stronger ties to its southern neighbors as a result.

Kentucky also suffered from the economic depression that overcame the South after the war. Many tobacco farmers went bankrupt. The state's hemp industry was especially hard hit. Before the Civil War, hemp fibers had been used for bags that held picked cotton, rope that tied cotton bales together, and rigging on sailing ships. After the war there wasn't much need for hemp. The war destroyed much of the South's cotton production, and steamships began to replace ships with sails. Plantation owners banded together to fight for laws that would help them, but recovery was slow.

Kentucky's economy started to improve in the last part of the nineteenth century. A major factor in the recovery was the new railroad lines that cut through the state. Kentucky products could now be shipped as far as the rail lines could take them. Kentucky coal, oil, and timber were shipped to areas that could afford them. Much of the state's coal was mined from two rich coal fields; one in western Kentucky and the other in the Appalachian Plateau. Underground mines accounted for over half of the coal produced. Tobacco became a leading crop in central and eastern areas of Kentucky. An increased interest in horse racing encouraged horse farmers to begin breeding expensive thoroughbreds. By 1890 the United States had 314 organized racetracks, and Kentucky horses were racing on most of them.

In the late 1800s and early 1900s, a small group of tobacco companies banded together to buy all the tobacco grown in Kentucky. By doing this the companies no longer had to compete with each other for the best price from farmers. As a group, the companies could pay the farmers whatever low price they wanted for tobacco. Some farmers fought back, however. They tried to persuade other tobacco farmers not to sell their tobacco at the low prices offered by the companies. From 1904 to 1909, farmers rode out at night burning the fields, barns, and warehouses of growers who sold to the companies. This action became known as the Black Patch War. At last the group of companies was broken up. Farmers created tobacco auctions to help sell their crops at fair prices.

Many other Kentucky workers had to fight for fair treatment, too. Clashes between coal mine owners and members of the United Mine Workers (UMW) became violent during the 1930s. The violence in Harlan County in the Appalachian Plateau region

A tobacco farmer in his field is watched by an armed guard during the Black Patch War.

This coal mine was once operated by the Proctor Coal Company. Coal has long been Kentucky's most valuable mineral resource.

was so bad that the county became known nationwide as "Bloody Harlan." The UMW wanted the owners to improve work conditions, shorten the workday, and pay higher wages.

Meanwhile another economic crisis hit Kentucky, along with the rest of the nation. The Great Depression of the 1930s forced thousands of people to become unemployed. Financial institutions failed and businesses went bankrupt. In 1933 the nation benefited from President Franklin D. Roosevelt's New Deal policies, which included construction projects. For example, the Tennessee Valley Authority (TVA) began construction on a steam-generating plant in southern Kentucky. Also, the Rural Electrification Administration (REA) made electricity available at low rates to rural Kentucky areas. New highways, factories, state and national parks, and Fort Knox were built in Kentucky during this time.

The beginning of World War II brought many people throughout the nation back into the workforce. Reopened factories began making materials for the war effort. Many people living in the rural areas in the 1940s moved to the industrial centers to look for jobs. Coal mines once again began supplying coal to factories. During World War II, the amount of the state's manufacturing increased by almost four times. The war also brought life back to many Kentucky farms. Modern farm machinery and improved farming techniques helped large plantations become more efficient than smaller farms that could not afford to modernize. The smaller farms were bought up and combined with the plantations.

During the late 1960s, Kentucky faced the same challenges in race relations as the rest of the country. In 1966 Kentucky was the first southern state to pass a comprehensive civil rights law. Many jobs and public facilities were opened to African Americans. School integration laws were finally passed in the 1970s despite strong opposition.

Kentucky made steps toward improving the quality of its education in 1989 with the establishment of a state lottery. A percentage of the profits provided by the lottery is set aside to fund the education system. The Education Reform Act of 1990 was designed to improve the quality of education in the state.

The state has always been able to count its leaders and abundant natural resources among its many advantages. That's why many people in Kentucky feel that the state will continue to improve with age.

One Family's Courage

A. D. Porter founded the family business.

A. D. Porter was a man of vision. He believed African American votes could change things. He also believed that the Democratic party would do more for African Americans than the Republicans could. But the Republican party was the party of Abraham Lincoln, who had freed the slaves.

So Porter had to fight against all those who disagreed with him, even his neighbors. Still, he raised his son Woodford to believe in the vote.

Woodford remembers when Louisville became violent. In the late 1920s, his father was supporting a Democrat for mayor. Woodford suffered a lot of grief for that. "I was pushed around, shoved around, called nasty names, knocked down," Woodford said. "Once someone rode by our house and fired a shot through our window. The bullet lodged about four or five feet above my head in the bed where I was sleeping. It wasn't a very pleasant time."

Today, Woodford says, involvement in politics is the best way to find better avenues for your community. "Everyone talks about political power, and there certainly is power in votes," he said.

The Porter family business is a mortuary, or funeral home, that serves the African American community. It was founded by A. D. Porter in 1907. Owning a business has given the family independence. They have not had to worry about losing jobs because of taking unpopular stands.

When the civil rights movement became strong in Kentucky in the 1960s, another generation of Porters stood up for what they believed. At that time African Americans were struggling against the political system. The Declaration of Independence said "all men are created equal," but African Americans did not have the same rights as other people. The national civil rights movement demanded those rights. Often these demands were stated through peaceful demonstrations, in which slogans were chanted. Woodford told his children to do what they felt was right and he would support them. His children were arrested a few times for taking part in organized protests.

Alongside their political struggles, the Porters have always carried on their business. Today, Woodford, Jr., known as "Woody," is a partner in the funeral home, and one of Woodford's granddaughters, Sasha, works there, too. The business has supported four generations of the Porter family.

The Porters have succeeded partly because of the strength and love they give to each other. Even if there's a risk, they support each other all the way.

"Woody" Woodford Porter, Jr., and his father, Woodford Porter, Sr., are partners in the family business.

Bluegrass Business

Kentucky is blessed with a rich and varied landscape. It has fertile farmlands and coal-rich mountains. Part of the state is forested, yet much of it consists of grassy meadows. The state's economy is as varied as its land. Kentucky is one of the few states with important manufacturing, agricultural, mining, and tourist industries.

The state's biggest financial problem is that, even though its economy is growing, too many people still have very low incomes. The per capita income in Kentucky is $16,534. This figure places Kentucky among the lowest ten of the fifty states. In Appalachia, the average family income is less than $15,000 a year. Appalachia refers to the area near the Appalachian Mountains in the eastern section of the state.

The economy is improving in Kentucky, however. Manufacturing is the leading economic activity. It began to edge out farming in importance right after the Civil War. Manufacturing has been growing ever since. The manufacturing industry accounts for almost

Bourbon whiskey takes its name from Bourbon County, where Jacob Spears distilled whiskey in 1790. Pictured here is the Old Taylor Distillery near Frankfort.

The world headquarters of Kentucky Fried Chicken is located in Kentucky. Many chickens are raised and sold in the state.

$18 billion in income every year in Kentucky. This amounts to about a quarter of the state's revenue.

The state's most valuable manufacturing activity is food production. This industry produces meats, poultry, baked goods, and beverages, including bourbon whiskey. Next comes transportation equipment, especially automobiles and auto parts. Kentucky has four major car factories and hundreds of companies that make automobile parts. The third most important manufacturing activity

One of the most popular sports cars in the United States is the Corvette. These robots are precision-welding a Corvette uniframe. The entire uniframe production area was automated in the early 1980s, just in time to produce the 1984 Corvette.

is the production of nonelectrical machinery. Kentucky factories also make air conditioning and heating equipment, farm machinery, typewriters, conveyors, and ball bearings.

In recent years the people of Kentucky have been successful in luring manufacturers to their state. Government officials say four factors set Kentucky apart from other states. The first is location. Factories in Kentucky are only one day's drive from seventy percent of the United States population. This means that they are in a prime position to reach the largest number of people with their manufactured goods. A second reason is that Kentucky has the least expensive electric power of any state east of the Rocky Mountains. Manufacturers like that because they know their electric costs will be as low as possible.

Another important consideration is the hard-work ethic of Kentucky's people. According to federal figures, the state's per-worker productivity is higher than any surrounding state. That means that Kentucky factories can do more work with fewer people than those in the other states. Finally, the state government actively seeks manufacturing business. Low taxes, especially in some areas, and efficient business methods make the state attractive to outside interests. The state government is especially interested in attracting businesses to the areas where many people are out of work.

Kentucky is still a leading coal-producing state. Coal mining is far less important to the economy than it once was, but it's still significant. Kentucky also supplies petroleum, limestone, and natural gas.

A worker seals a bottle of Maker's Mark whiskey.

Even though machines are being used more and more, a great deal of Kentucky's finest tobacco is still harvested the traditional way.

Kentucky's swift thorough-bred horses are probably the state's best-known product.

Agriculture remains an important part of life in Kentucky, also. The economy no longer depends on tobacco farming as it did shortly after the Civil War. Tobacco is still the state's largest cash crop, however. In fact, Kentucky is the second most important tobacco-growing state in the country. Other crops include apples, soybeans, corn, and wheat. Dairy products, hogs, eggs, and young chickens are also important agricultural products.

Central Kentucky has prime grazing land for livestock. In Kentucky when you talk about livestock, you're talking about horses. Kentucky has been famous for breeding horses for more than two centuries. Once, these animals were used only for transportation and hauling. Today, the horses are thorough-breds, primarily used for running in races. Horses aren't the only animals raised on Kentucky farms, though. Beef cattle bring in about as much income as horses do.

People traditionally like to spend their vacations outdoors among beautiful scenery. More and more, they want to spend it close to home. Kentucky is close to home for a lot of people. In fact, it borders seven states. Overall, the tourist income in Kentucky more than tripled during the early 1990s. Vacationers and business travelers bring in more than $6 billion each year. The famous horse farms of the central bluegrass area are one of the main attractions. Tourists are also attracted to the Appalachian Mountains for camping, biking, and hiking. The wooded hills and low mountains of eastern Kentucky are among the most beautiful areas in the United States.

The image of elegant thoroughbred horses grazing quietly on Kentucky bluegrass, or thundering around a racetrack, is certainly the primary allure of Kentucky. The state's mind may be on business, but its heart remains with its most famous animal.

Kentucky Fried Chicken is popular in the United States and in more than three thousand locations worldwide.

Horse Sense

You just cannot tell people about Kentucky without talking about horses and horse racing. From the bluegrass farms where they're raised to the Kentucky Derby where they're raced, Kentucky's passion is sleek, thoroughbred horses.

That's the way it's been for more than two centuries. Not long after explorers crossed the Appalachian Mountains, settlers moved into central Kentucky. The rich river valleys and lush grasslands there provided perfect grazing land for horses. At that time, roughly the 1780s, horses were used to help with the farm work and for transportation. They pulled wagons, carriages, and plows. The settlers occasionally liked to race their favorite horses, too. The first horse races in Kentucky were private contests between the horses of two owners on a makeshift track.

Horse racing, in the meantime, had become a very popular sport in Great Britain. The British were racing horses on permanent tracks with professional riders. As more British came to America in the early 1800s, they brought their enthusiasm for professional horse racing with them.

Racehorse owners quickly discovered that the strong, fast horses bred on the Kentucky pastures seemed to have a natural advantage. Thoroughbred ranches started popping up all over central Kentucky. From that day to this, most of this country's finest racehorses have come from the Bluegrass State. Of course, other places have produced great horses, but nowhere near the number that have come from Kentucky.

It is only natural, then, that the most famous horse race in the United States is held in Kentucky. The Kentucky Derby was first held in 1875 at Churchill Downs racetrack in Louisville. It's been held there every spring since then. The race is so popular that hotel rooms in Louisville are completely sold out for race weekend more than six months ahead of time. Out of the 120 Derbys that have been run, 89 have been won by Kentucky horses!

The Taylor family is right there in the middle of the horse business. They live in Nicholasville, just south of

For 120 years, the Kentucky Derby in Louisville has drawn race fans from all over the country.

Lexington and about 70 miles east of Louisville. Joe Taylor was general manager at Gainesway for more than thirty years. Gainesway is one of the top horse farms in the world. Joe Taylor, himself the son of a horseman, has been instrumental to its success. Today, Joe's four sons have created their own family farm. It's called Taylor Made Farm & Sales Agency. The Taylor family breeds, boards, and sells horses at auction.

There is big money to be made racing and breeding winning horses. A champion is worth many millions of dollars, and some owners buy horses for just that reason. They regard the animals as an opportunity to get rich.

Those who own the farms and work on them, however, feel the

business is more than just a way to make money. It's truly a labor of love.

"We knew we wanted to be in the horse business. We always knew that," said Mark Taylor, one of Joe's sons. "The horse business had always been the business our father had been in. We've always wanted to please him, and so we just followed in his footsteps, trying to do the best we can."

The best the Taylor boys can do is pretty good. Ben, Duncan, Frank, and Mark started by boarding a few mares. Now they've built a reputation as an outstanding sales agency for thoroughbred yearlings, horses between one and two years old. Since the 1,200-acre farm was started in 1976, it has sold more than $175 million worth of horses at public auctions. But no matter how successful the farm becomes, it remains a labor of love.

Joe Taylor puts it this way: "The horse is my favorite animal. I don't dislike a dog or a cat. But I think a

Ben, Duncan, Frank, Joe, and Mark Taylor appear with one of their horses.

horse shows enough emotion that I just like to be around them. They're thankful for what you do for them."

It's easy to do a good job when you love what you do. The Taylor family is living proof of that.

The Taylors show a horse to some possible buyers.

Horses at the Taylor farm receive only the best food and care.

The Art of the Country

Over the years, the United States grew from a small collection of colonies to become a vast nation. State boundaries were formed, industry became mechanized, and people from all over the world arrived to raise families. One thing people brought with them when they came to the United States was their culture. Over the years, the various cultural forms blended together. But some groups did not grow and change with the rest of the country. One group of people lived in a world apart. They lived in an area where the landscape was rugged and hard to cross. Few roads were available, and for years hardly anyone traveled to or from the area. This hidden, mysterious place was an area called Appalachia. Part of this area is in the eastern region of Kentucky.

The people of Appalachia did not become part of our nation's melting pot. They continued to sing the songs their ancestors brought with them from England. They kept speaking a language that had its roots in fifteenth-century England. They told the folktales and

The Kentucky Derby is held at Churchill Downs every year on the first Saturday in May. The tradition dates back to 1875.

Quilting by hand is a process requiring many hours of painstaking labor. This woman is sewing a pieced quilt, which uses several pieces of cloth to form a design.

made the kind of crafts that were long forgotten by the rest of the country.

Roads leading into Appalachia were built in the 1920s. As Appalachian people came into contact with outsiders, the Appalachian arts became less pure. But the culture of this mountain region still has a special quality. The people of Appalachia in eastern Kentucky still make their furniture by hand. They also carefully and lovingly stitch their quilts from remnants of old clothes.

The Appalachian Mountains are the original source of what eventually became bluegrass music. It's music for dancing—if your feet can move that fast. The fiddles sing and the banjos dazzle. When the first outsiders came into this

During the 1700s and early 1800s, all furniture was made by hand. Kentucky crafts-people have preserved that tradition. This man is working on a rocking chair.

area, they were amazed to find people playing and singing songs that the outside world thought had been lost for centuries. Often, the musicians played on homemade instruments. Around the 1920s, musicologists and historians brought tape recorders and captured the mountain music. Today, the whole world can share this priceless musical heritage.

There's another side to Kentucky culture, one that has strong ties to the plantation life of the South. These ties show up in many different ways. For example, one of America's great writers lived and wrote in Kentucky. Robert Penn Warren was a three-time Pulitzer Prize winner. His best-known novel, *All the King's Men*, was based on the life of Louisiana's Governor Huey Long. Another well-known Kentucky writer was Harriette Simpson Arnow. She wrote *The Dollmaker*, a story about a woman living in the poorest part of Appalachia. William Wells Brown, a Kentuckian, was this country's first African American to publish a novel. He was also the first African

This is the interior of White Hall in Richmond. White Hall belonged to the father of Cassius Marcellus Clay. Clay was a famous abolitionist, publisher, and minister to Russia. He was also a friend of Abraham Lincoln.

This Native American outfit was worn by John James Audubon in the early 1800s. It is part of an exhibit at the John James Audubon Museum at Audubon State Park, near Henderson. Audubon lived in Henderson in the early 1800s.

American to publish a drama and the first to publish a travel book.

Another link to the South is songwriter Stephen Foster. His songs were immensely popular just before the Civil War. Though he was not born in Kentucky, he lived there during part of his life. One of his most beautiful and moving songs, "My Old Kentucky Home," was written about a house that still stands near Bardstown, in central Kentucky.

Kentucky's attachment to the past is strong, and rural life is an important part of its culture even today. But it would be a big mistake to think Kentucky's culture does not reside in the cities, too.

Louisville has an outstanding symphony orchestra, a ballet troupe, and an excellent art museum. The Actors Theater of Louisville became Kentucky's state theater in 1974. Every year thousands of plays are submitted to the Louisville Playwriting Competition. It is one of the most important playwriting competitions in the world. Then people from all over the country gather in Louisville to see fine productions of these new plays.

Other parts of the state have much to offer, as well. In Shelbyville, the Wakefield-Scearce Galleries contain one of the world's outstanding collections of antiques. Many original paintings by John James

Audubon, the famous painter of wild birds, are displayed in a new museum in Audubon State Park, near Henderson. In Frankfort, the state capital, Luscher's Museum of the American Farmer showcases two hundred years of farm tools and machinery.

Kentucky does not neglect the outdoor pleasures. Its gently rolling hills and quiet forests offer countless opportunities for hiking and camping. Like many of its neighboring states, Kentucky has built dams across some of its rivers. These dams were constructed to generate electric power. They also create lovely lakes. It's hard to imagine a more tranquil vacation than renting a houseboat and cruising along the wooded shore of a quiet lake.

In its culture as well as in many other areas, Kentuckians have maintained a difficult balance. They honor and respect their past as a kind of living history. Yet at the same time, they have created a modern state ready for life in the twenty-first century.

The legendary racehorse Man O' War won all but one of his races, which he lost to a horse named Upset. This statue of Man O' War stands in Kentucky Horse Park, where Man O' War's grave is located.

Kentucky Musical Traditions

When the first colonists came through the Cumberland Gap and began to settle throughout the hills and mountains of eastern Kentucky, they brought their music with them. And in that rugged, hard-to-reach part of the state, the music stayed unchanged—and undiscovered—for about 150 years.

Another thing that didn't change was the close-knit family bonds. "A family in the Kentucky mountains, especially in eastern Kentucky, means your clan," says singer and musician Jean Ritchie. "Our family is scattered all over the country now. But still, if ever there's a call that goes out and says, 'We're going to get together,' everybody'll break their necks to get here."

Jean Ritchie, the youngest of fourteen children, knows all about hill-country families and the music they play. She was born in 1922 in the tiny town of Viper, in the Cumberland Mountains of southeastern Kentucky. She recalls that when she was a child,

"Viper was a tiny village whose fifteen or twenty houses string out like a chain around the hillside where it dips inward to follow the curve of the river." Even today, the town has a population of only several hundred.

In those remote hills, in the days before cable television, families would gather and sing as a principal form of entertainment. From her childhood, Jean Ritchie learned hundreds of traditional Scotch, Irish, and English songs. They dated back to when her ancestor James Ritchie and his five brothers came to America from Scotland in 1768.

Ms. Ritchie has performed the songs she learned as a child all over the world. She has recorded more than thirty albums and written ten books. She was a founder of the Newport Folk Festival.

Meanwhile, a young man named Bill Monroe was growing up in western Kentucky. He learned to play the guitar, the violin (which country folk call a fiddle), and a stringed instrument called a mandolin. It looks a little like a very small guitar with a rounded back. In 1938 Bill Monroe formed his first band, which he called the Blue Grass

Jean Ritchie's family is as numerous as her song recordings. Ritchie is the youngest of 14 children.

Boys in honor of his state's nickname. Within a year, Monroe's band was playing on the "Grand Ole Opry," a country music radio program. The Opry was broadcast live from Nashville, Tennessee, every Saturday night. It was one of the most popular shows in the country.

The music Bill Monroe was playing was a little different from the pure folk ballads of Jean Ritchie. His music was born from the same roots, however. Unlike Jean Ritchie's Appalachian music, Monroe's bluegrass music was changed by outside influences, including blues and gospel music.

Bill Monroe and the Blue Grass Boys gave their name to a whole style of music. Now nearly everyone has heard of bluegrass music. The music went through a decline in the 1950s and 1960s. Its fans were growing older, and young people didn't want to hear anything but rock 'n' roll. However, the folk music revival of the 1960s, and country music's renewed popularity in the 1970s and 1980s, has brought bluegrass back into the spotlight.

Bluegrass is a unique American kind of music. It's not folk and not country, although it has elements of both. But however you classify it, there's no doubt that it's now more popular than ever. There are more than six hundred bluegrass

Bill Monroe has been strumming and fiddling since 1936— almost fifty years.

music festivals every year in the United States alone. Bluegrass also has thousands of enthusiastic fans in both Europe and Japan. Bill Monroe, now over eighty years old, is still playing to packed houses.

The old Kentucky values of love of land and family are continuing in the music of Jean Ritchie and Bill Monroe and all their followers. Those traditions, and that love, are part of what it means to be from Kentucky. It's what always brings Jean Ritchie back.

"They always say you can't go home again," Ms. Ritchie said. "Somebody wrote that in a book and everybody seems to think that makes it absolutely true. But it's not. You can go home again, and I've done it. And I love it here. I've traveled all around the world, but I still love this place better than any other."

Jean Ritchie gave the Appalachian dulcimer, the instrument she is playing in this photo, its name.

Bluegrass star Alison Krauss became very popular when she opened several concerts for country singer Garth Brooks.

In the Dark

You're walking through an underground passageway. It's dark and completely silent except for the sound of your breathing and your footsteps. You should be scared, but you're not. In fact, you're having the time of your life. You're journeying through Mammoth Cave.

At first it may seem like there are no other living things in the cave. After all, this is an environment made of rock, a place without sunlight. You might be surprised to learn that there are more than two hundred animal species in Mammoth Cave. These creatures are part of what makes the cave such a special place. The number of animals there rivals that of any cave region in the world. Some of the animals, such as raccoons and bullfrogs, just wander in by accident. They often stay only the time it takes them to find their way out again. But then there are cave dwellers, too. They're called troglobites—animals that have adapted themselves to living without light. And they're a pretty strange bunch. Some have no eyes. Years of living in the dark has eliminated their

This park ranger at Mammoth Cave National Park is explaining to visitors the amazing sights they are about to see inside the caves.

need for eyesight. However, most troglobites have developed very sensitive hearing and touch. This helps protect them from predators. It also allows them to find food in a place where food is scarce. Because the cave is so dark, some animals have lost the need for the skin coloring that protects them from the sun. These animals appear white or transparent.

What other creatures live in the cave? Some are trogloxenes, or cave visitors. They live in the cave but go outside to find food. Some well-known trogloxenes are bats and crickets. Twelve species of bats occupy Mammoth Cave. But the cave's bat population is not large. If you visit

Mammoth Caves, you're much more likely to see cave crickets than bats.

It's a mysterious world inside Mammoth Cave. Its 345 miles of underground passageways will always provide plenty to explore. While you're there, look around closely. You might feel as if you're alone. But you'll know you're not.

This is Mammoth Cave's Frozen Niagara. Mammoth Cave is the second oldest tourist attraction in the United States; Niagara Falls is the oldest.

The Mammoth Cave system is the longest system of caves in the world.

41

Taking Care of the Family— and the Future

Kentucky is a place of great beauty and rich natural resources. Its people are hard working and as rugged as the hills. Yet one of Kentucky's greatest challenges for the future is to provide these people with more of what they need for a good life.

For too many years, the Appalachian region was dependent on the coal-mining industry. The coal mines provided jobs, but they were dangerous and low paying. Today, machines have made the jobs less dangerous. The pay is much better, as well. But there are fewer jobs available. Kentucky's coal industry enjoyed a burst of prosperity during the 1970s. The petroleum shortage and sharply rising prices greatly increased the demand for coal. But once the crisis eased, the coal industry went back into decline. Today, the Appalachian region would benefit from new industries and new sources of income for its people.

The farmers, too, are going to have to find new sources of income. More and more, farming is being replaced by "agribusiness." Major grain, soybean, and

Louisville is a modern city on the banks of the Ohio River. It is home to the University of Louisville, Spalding University, and Bellarmine College.

The Louisville Galleria is a modern shopping mall in a modern city.

livestock producers are more in evidence today than small tobacco farmers. For farmers, the answer may lie in industry. Kentucky has been successful in attracting manufacturers. The state's tax benefits encourage companies to locate where the most people need jobs. In many cases, these are the areas where small farmers have been bought out by big farming corporations. If Kentucky's growth as an industrial state continues, there may someday be jobs for everyone.

To meet the challenges of the twenty-first century, Kentucky is overhauling its educational system. The Kentucky Education Reform Act (KERA) was passed in 1990. Within five years, the plan will have revised school lessons to emphasize development of thinking skills, not just learning facts. Tutoring, day care, and health care services will be available for children who need them. Computerized and video learning aids will also be used. Another resource for teaching children is the Kentucky Educational Television network. It is the largest such network in the nation.

Clearly, Kentucky is serious about making sure its people won't be left behind by our fast-changing world! It is working today to build a secure tomorrow.

Important Historical Events

1750 Dr. Thomas Walker explores the area and names the Cumberland Gap.

1767 Daniel Boone makes his first trip into Kentucky.

1773 Boone tries to bring in a group of settlers. They are turned back by Native Americans.

1774 Native Americans lose their rights to all land south of the Ohio River to Virginia. James Harrod founds the first permanent European settlement in Kentucky.

1775 The Cherokee sell their rights in the area to the Transylvania Company.

1776 Kentucky becomes part of Fincastle County of Virginia and then becomes Kentucky County.

1778 George Rogers Clark defeats the French, Native Americans, and British at Kaskaskia, Cahokia, and Vincennes.

1782 Native Americans defeat the settlers at Blue Licks in the last major battle between Native Americans and settlers in Kentucky.

1784 The settlers hold the first of nine conventions to consider separating from Virginia.

1792 Kentucky becomes the fifteenth state.

1816 Mammoth Cave is first promoted as a tourist attraction.

1817 The first Beethoven symphony ever heard in the United States is presented in Lexington.

1833 Kentucky passes a law that no more slaves can be brought in.

1861 The Civil War begins, and Kentucky attempts to remain neutral.

1870 Farmers begin growing burley tobacco in central and eastern Kentucky.

1875 The first Kentucky Derby is run.

1904 The Black Patch War begins in western Kentucky.

1936 Fort Knox is opened.

1962 State legislature passes laws regulating strip mining of coal.

1966 Kentucky is the first southern state to pass a comprehensive civil rights law.

1969 The Tennessee Valley Authority completes its largest steam-generating plant.

1978 The Kentucky state legislature passes a law stating that strip miners must restore the land as nearly as possible to its original condition.

1988 A Toyota factory opens in Georgetown; it will employ more than six thousand workers by 1995.

1990 The Kentucky Education Reform Act (KERA) is passed.

The flag shows a frontiersman and a statesman embracing, surrounded by the words *United We Stand, Divided We Fall.* Goldenrod, the state flower, and the words *Commonwealth of Kentucky* encircle the two figures. The blue field and the gold are the state's official colors.

Kentucky Almanac

Nickname. The Bluegrass State

Capital. Frankfort

State Bird. Kentucky cardinal

State Flower. Goldenrod

State Tree. Tulip poplar

State Motto. United We Stand, Divided We Fall

State Song. "My Old Kentucky Home"

State Abbreviations. Ky. or Ken. (traditional); KY (postal)

Statehood. June 1, 1792, the 15th state

Government. Congress: U.S. senators, 2; U.S. representatives, 6. State Legislature: senators, 38; representatives, 100. Counties: 120

Area. 40,395 sq mi (104,623 sq km), 37th in size among the states

Greatest Distances. north/south, 175 mi (282 km); east/west, 350 mi (563 km)

Elevation. Highest: Black Mountain, 4,139 ft (1,262 m). Lowest: 257 ft (78 m)

Population. 1990 Census: 3,685,296 (0.6% increase over 1980), 23rd among the states. Density: 92.3 persons per sq mi (35 persons per sq km). Distribution: 51% urban, 49% rural. 1980 Census: 3,661,433

Economy. *Agriculture:* beef cattle, horses, tobacco, soybeans, hogs, chickens, corn, wheat. *Manufacturing:* food products, transportation equipment, nonelectrical machinery, electrical equipment, tobacco products. *Mining:* coal, natural gas, petroleum, limestone

State Seal

State Flower: Goldenrod

State Bird: Kentucky cardinal

Annual Events

★ Winter Weekends at Shaker Village, near Harrodsburg (January/February)

★ Festival of New American Plays in Louisville (March/April)

★ International Bar-B-Q Festival in Owensboro (May)

★ Kentucky Derby in Louisville (first Saturday in May)

★ Capital Expo in Frankfort (June)

★ Festival of the Bluegrass in Lexington (June)

★ State Fair in Louisville (August)

★ Bluegrass American Music Festival in Louisville (September)

★ Kentucky Highlands Folk Festival in Prestonburg (September)

★ Kentucky Guild of Artists and Craftsmen's Fair in Berea (October)

★ Lincoln Days Celebration in Hodgenville (October)

Places to Visit

★ Bluegrass Music Museum and Hall of Fame in Owensboro

★ Breaks Interstate Park, Sandy River, near Elkhorn City

★ Cumberland Gap National Historical Park in southeastern Kentucky

★ Fort Knox, near Louisville

★ John James Audubon Memorial Museum, near Henderson

★ Kentucky Derby Museum in Louisville

★ Kentucky Historical Society in Frankfort

★ Kentucky Horse Park in Lexington

★ Liberty Hall in Frankfort

★ Lincoln's birthplace, near Hodgenville

★ Mammoth Cave National Park, 90 miles south of Louisville

★ Shaker Village at Pleasant Hill, near Lexington

47

Index